Celebrate the Season

Cathy Marie Hake

DayMaker
GREETING BOOKS

Dashing through the snow?

*Wondering which will give out first—
your feet or your budget?*

Christmas isn't supposed to be
a marathon of exhausting obligations—
it's a celebration of all that is good and right
because of the first Gift given in Bethlehem.

Celebrate the Season!

Good news from heaven the angels bring,
Glad tidings to the earth they sing:
To us this day a child is given,
To crown us with the joy of heaven.

MARTIN LUTHER

Deck the halls. . .

Boughs of holly,
Swags of pine,
Festive red ribbons
And parcels wrapped in twine.
Garland and tinsel,
Candles glowing bright,
Star-shaped cookies,
And strings of lights,
Christmas ornaments of red, white, and green,
But the best decorations are the loved ones
   we've seen.

*Perhaps the best Yuletide decoration is
being wreathed in smiles.*

UNKNOWN

'Tis the season to be jolly. . .

It is requisite for the relaxation of the mind
that we make use, from time to time,
of playful deeds and jokes.

St. Thomas Aquinas

*In things pertaining to enthusiasm,
no man is sane who does not know how
to be insane on proper occasions.*

Henry Ward Beecher

Fa la la la la. . .

Music has charms to soothe the savage breast
To soften rocks, or bend a knotted oak.

WILLIAM CONGREVE

Unwind. Relax. Set the mood for your holiday season by surrounding yourself with music. Hum. Sing. Listen to carols in the car. Go caroling and share the joy!

Let's dance and sing and make good cheer,
For Christmas comes but once a year.

Sir George Alexander MacFarren

Celebrate the holidays in dozens of small ways.
Joy has a way of multiplying.

Make the most of the season.
Share it with the ones you love!

Love came down at Christmas,
Love all lovely, Love Divine;
Love was born at Christmas;
Star and angels gave the sign.

CHRISTINA ROSSETTI

Love is the best reason to
celebrate. Carry that attitude
all year long!

I will honor Christmas in my heart,
and try to keep it all the year.

EBENEEZER SCROOGE,
in *A Christmas Carol* BY CHARLES DICKENS

Christmas Eve was a night of song that
wrapped itself about you like a shawl. But it
warmed more than your body. It warmed your
heart. . .filled it, too, with a melody that would
last forever.

BESS STREETER ALDRICH

Christians awake,
salute the happy morn
whereon the Savior of the world was born.

JOHN BYROM

Two things upon this changing earth
can neither change nor end;
the splendor of Christ's humble birth,
the love of friend for friend.

UNKNOWN

*Christmas is the season for
kindling the fire of hospitality in the hall,
the genial flame of charity in the heart.*

WASHINGTON IRVING

Our hearts grow tender with childhood memories and love of kindred, and we are better throughout the year for having, in spirit, become a child again at Christmastime.

LAURA INGALLS WILDER

Happy, happy Christmas, that can win us back to the delusions of our childish days; that can recall to the old man the pleasures of his youth; that can transport the sailor and the traveler, thousands of miles away, back to his own fireside and his quiet home!

CHARLES DICKENS

The magi, as you know, were wise men—wonderfully wise men who brought gifts to the Babe in the manger. They invented the art of giving Christmas presents.

O. HENRY

The joy of brightening other lives, bearing each others' burdens, easing others' loads, and supplanting empty hearts and lives with generous gifts becomes for us the magic of Christmas.

W. C. JONES

The best present is the gift of
a family around a glittering tree,
wrapped in contentment
and tied with a ribbon of charity.

Somehow, not only for Christmas,
But all the long year through,
The joy that you give to others,
Is the joy that comes back to you.
And the more you spend in blessing,
The poor and lonely and sad,
The more of your heart's possessing,
Returns to you glad.

JOHN GREENLEAF WHITTIER

Let
us re-
member
that
the
Christmas heart is a giving heart,
a wide-open heart that thinks of
others first. The birth of the baby
Jesus stands as the most signifi-
cant event in all history, because
it has meant the pouring into a
sick world of the healing medicine
of love which has transformed all
manner of hearts for almost two
thousand years. . . . Underneath all
the bulging bundles is this beating
Christmas heart. — GEORGE MATTHEW ADAMS

The first gift
of Christmas was self.
Christ gave us Himself
to light the way to heaven.

To give without any reward,
or any notice,
has a special quality of its own.

ANNE MORROW LINDBERGH

Remember
This December,
That love weighs more than gold!

JOSEPHINE DODGE DASKAM BACON

A Christmas Blessing:

During this Christmas season,
May you be blessed
With the spirit of the season,
Which is peace,
The gladness of the season,
Which is hope,
And the heart of the season,
Which is love.

One of the nice things about Christmas is that you can make people forget the past with a present!

ANONYMOUS

The best gifts don't fit neatly into a box. Forgive someone; you'll free yourself. Show kindness; you'll find joy. Respect others and you'll cultivate self-esteem. In giving, we ultimately discover treasures within. Carry on the celebration of giving all the year long.

It is more blessed to give than to receive!

I think I began learning long ago that those who are happiest are those who do the most for others.

BOOKER T. WASHINGTON

We must want for others,
not ourselves alone.

ELEANOR ROOSEVELT

You make a living by what you get, but you make a life by what you give.

UNKNOWN

If there is no joyous way to give a festive gift,
give love away.

UNKNOWN

May peace be your gift at Christmas
and your blessing all year through!

UNKNOWN

For little children everywhere
A joyous season still we make;
We bring our precious gifts to them,
Even for the dear child Jesus' sake.

PHOEBE CARY

Joy is not in things;
it is in us.

RICHARD WAGNER

Open yourself to the fun of the season.
Appreciate the refreshing spirit of kindness.
Laugh and enjoy everything around you.

The sun does not shine
for a few trees and flowers,
but for the wide world's joy.

HENRY WARD BEECHER

Reflect upon your present blessings—
of which every man has many—
not on your past misfortunes,
of which all men have some.

CHARLES DICKENS

No duty is more urgent
than that of returning thanks.

ANONYMOUS

Blessed is the season
which engages the whole world in
a conspiracy of love.

HAMILTON WRIGHT MABI

Christmas is not a time nor a season, but a state of mind. To cherish peace and goodwill, to be plenteous in mercy, is to have the real spirit of Christmas.

CALVIN COOLIDGE

Until one feels the spirit of Christmas,
there is no Christmas.
All else is outward display—
so much tinsel and decorations.
For it isn't the holly, it isn't the snow.
It isn't the tree, not the firelight's glow.
It's the warmth that comes
to the hearts of men
when the Christmas spirit returns again.

UNKNOWN

Time was with most of us, when Christmas Day, encircling all our limited world like a magic ring, left nothing out for us to miss or seek; bound together all our home enjoyments, affections, and hopes; grouped everything and everyone 'round the Christmas fire, and made the picture shining in our bright young eyes complete.

CHARLES DICKENS

Christmas—that magic blanket that wraps
itself about us, that something so intangible
that it is like a fragrance. It may weave a
spell of nostalgia. Christmas may be a day of
feasting or prayer, but always it will be a day
of remembrance—a day in which we think of
everything we have ever loved.

AUGUSTA E. RUNDEL

*Christmas is the day
that holds time together.*

ALEXANDER

Joy to the world! The Lord is come:
Let earth receive her King!

And the angel said unto them, Fear not: for, behold,
I bring you good tidings of great joy, which shall be
to all people. For unto you is born this day in the
city of David a Saviour, which is Christ the Lord.
And this shall be a sign unto you; Ye shall find
the babe wrapped in swaddling clothes, lying in a
manger.

LUKE 2:10–12

Let every heart prepare Him room,
And heaven and nature sing. . .

Are you willing to believe that love is the strongest thing in the world—stronger than hate, stronger than evil, stronger than death—and that the blessed life which began in Bethlehem nineteen hundred years ago is the image and brightness of Eternal Love? Then you can keep Christmas.

HENRY VAN DYKE

God rest ye merry, gentlemen,
Let nothing you dismay. . .

Where charity stands watching and faith holds
wide the door the dark night wakes—the glory
breaks, Christmas comes once more.

PHILLIPS BROOKS

Remember Christ our Savior
Was born on Christmas Day,
To save us all from Satan's pow'r
When we were gone astray:
O tidings of comfort and joy,
Comfort and joy. . .

When it is dark enough,
you can see the stars.

CHARLES A. BEARD

Whatever else be lost among the years,
let us keep Christmas still a shining thing:
Whatever doubts assail us, or what fears,
Let us hold close one day,
remembering its poignant meaning
for the hearts of men.
Let us get back our childlike faith again.

GRACE NOLL CROWELL

Merry Christmas!